For Catherine, Mom, Dad, Molly, the Hendrys and all of those who cared to teach me.

Moments are like rubber bands. I will keep stretching the ones we share.

Contents

Preface

Part I: The Wanderings

Preface

The metaphorical journey described in *The Nomad* was made possible by my friends and family, my community and backbone during the darkest and brightest parts of my life. In each passing year, they have showed me that even the simplest of conversations can unlock the inner workings of the universe, an experience I sought to replicate in these poems. It is also made possible by Dante Alighieri and TS Eliot, who I have walked beside in words and whose work advised me on the structure and style of *The Nomad*. The Nomad's epic journey through what we know as the modern world and its themes would not be possible without my knowledge of the distinction between harmful disorderly love and revitalizing orderly love. I can thank Alighieri and Eliot for making this distinction. This work of poetry is a product of organizing and shaping the love and passion of my life into a concrete form. I feel it is the closest I have come to giving shape to truth in my life thus far. The Nomad could have experienced life in any number of ways, but only one led him towards the true way, which is to love and live with all your heart, soul, and mind. This series of poems is divided into three parts which outline The Nomad's progression from childhood, adolescence, and to mature adulthood. His maturity is a result of evolving thoughts; thoughts which sometimes sing with each other and at other times, conflict. But they cannot be mistaken for anything else but poetry: For this is its nature and form. The epic journey of *The Nomad* is my personal proof that not all those who wander are lost, and those who take the chance to experience life in all of its colors of emotion and perspective truly live a meaningful life. I thank all of those who continue to read and may the road of experience stretch long before you.

Midway upon the journey of our life
  I found myself within a forest dark,
  For the straightforward pathway had been lost.

Ah me! how hard a thing it is to say
  What was this forest savage, rough, and stern,
  Which in the very thought renews the fear.

So bitter is it, death is little more;
  But of the good to treat, which there I found,
  Speak will I of the other things I saw there.

I cannot well repeat how there I entered,
  So full was I of slumber at the moment
  In which I had abandoned the true way.
  — Dante Alighieri (1265-1321 AD), Inferno

Part I
The Wanderings

The Nomad

I am going to a place without a familiar face!

With a loving stare stands a girl so fair...

She has stars and galaxies in her hair.

If only she could know me through telepathy

Or better yet, through empathy.

I leave this place without a familiar face!

I leave her loving stare, that girl so fair.

If only she could know me

Not through sympathy

But rather, in true community.

But I am alone.

Traveling without reason, without chase

The lowest of desires control my pace.

It is true, I am free

Unshackled from an ideal I cannot be.

But my soul is in anarchy,

My heart is lost.

My thoughts are scattered,

My body pays the cost.

I travel far and wide

In search of purpose, from duty I hide.

I have no responsibilities

And of that, strangely, I am glad.

But should I be?

I am too proud to confess a sin

I would not know where to begin.

Am I wrong? Am I right?

Which morals and truths are worth the fight?

Trapped in my mind

My thoughts meander.

In its dark cavern

I behold its grandeur.

I travel from place to place

Without reason, without chase.

Silence

There is a wall around me made of silence.

It cannot be broken

Unless for a token,

One of appreciation

Would create awareness and sensation.

Like a machine that takes money,

The token produces something funny.

I reach into you, your thoughts become mine.

I lift you up, like a glass of red wine.

I speak to you, and everything I say is true,

I make love enwrap you through and through.

But what results from our touch

Costs so much.

To break the silence

Would corrupt my self defense,

Create consequence

Make sounds in sequence.

Make patterns and shapes

Ourselves recorded on video tapes.

You speak, I listen

For a moment our souls glisten.

With effort and time,

Our voices and bodies can entwine.

Good Grief!

So much meaning I cannot handle,

I prefer to sit at a dinner table

Lit by a single candle.

And yet I know,

What is not spoken cannot be understood.

What is not done is only what should.

The Scream

People are like question marks
They mope through the street
Looking for answers
To bring them to their feet.

Shops, stops, stalls, and halls
They'll always be around.
Over, under, sunder, sunder
Their random ways, make me shudder.

I alone can hear them scream
Their torment quelled by my stare,
Pushing me away
As I gasp for air.

Behind their gaze is tension
A fear of most hideous invention.
This emotion is directed at me,
It is paranoia of the highest degree.

In whom no one to confide

I turn, run and hide.

An outsider I am destined to be

In the walls of this screaming city.

Gazing down from the safety of my room

To the horror that lurks below

I remind myself again and again,

Stay low my friend, stay low.

The Machine

I am caught between cogs,

Sophistication I cannot understand.

Massive trucks and trains

And flying airplanes

Surround me,

Like circus clowns.

It's as if I am trapped in a toolbox.

But the tools have no use,

They are just abuse.

Trees and fields plowed over by concrete,

Fleet upon fleet

Of trucks.

Criss cross the highways of my mind.

Tools, like computers, I know how to use,

But cannot make.

Even the pen I write with,

I cannot comprehend or recreate.

I can only make sensation,

Only feelings.

I am a consumer of sensation,

My one desire is sensation.

The machine,

You can hear its roar and fury,

Driving us towards sensation

Forcing growth.

Growth without reflection or direction,

Like a cancer.

I talk to machines

With my hands.

Using and abusing them.

Everything directed towards the self.

Without reciprocation,

Just for my own sensation.

The Questions

For all of the answers I know,

There are questions to be made;

Things that are expected to be asked about life.

My grave approaches me everyday

 And so I ask the questions now.

Why do the stars shine upon this dark world?

Why does the moonlight dance upon my bare skin?

Where do the roads end and the amazing journeys begin?

Where does time begin to curve,

And who do I serve?

Around these questions I continue to swerve

How is it that I came to be a moving body above

a barren rock?

I walk upon it,

Thinking and brooding without concluding.

I do not care to know,

I only ask the questions.

For these questions there are answers,

But right now,

I can only see beauty in bar hall dancers.

There is beauty in logic...

But it is so boring.

These questions may be the flares of futility.

The fading light of my own fertility.

If they are not answered, then who?

Who will take up the responsibility of my continuation?

Who will help prolong my awareness and sensation?

There is an inherent duty to remake my own

creation.

To answer my questions

Then they will be answered again and again.

The burden of each question

Leads to a raining depression.

The sky begins to cry.

I look at it and sigh.

The rain streaks the swirling sky.

Upon my head the drops lie,

Just like the questions.

My Religion

In regards to my God...

I have none.

What is my soul to become?

Will I wander in a sort of purgatory for endless

days?

Trying to find my way out in endless ways?

Maybe the better option is to believe

So that my soul can breathe.

To wander about is my wish,

To roam free in the open like a fish.

To contemplate this life without meaning,

Free from any thought too demeaning.

My self-esteem is like an inflated balloon.

Others watch and gloat, thinking it will pop soon.

For now I ride this high,

And rise up happily into the sky.

Who knows what I might see,

Maybe a god who looks like me.

What faith I had

Was lost in translation.

I can only make it up in conversation.

Sin

I would not know where to begin in regards to my sin.

I do know that every one I made

Was due to a mistake,

And I committed the sin to compensate.

There is something divine in thinking you'll be fine.

But there is said to be an impending doom

When your actions cross the line.

And yes I do live in fear of things I don't know.

But why stop the show?

Why stop the mistakes and apply the brakes?

Why stop the sauntering and loitering of my soul?

 I place myself above things I cannot control.

My actions push unceasingly in one direction

And only the best do I review in reflection.

Chocolate

Eating chocolate is like a dark brown kiss

It is my nourishment of nightly bliss.

It is the most precious food that I hoard

My decadent and brittle Overlord.

 It is the lode of sweet seduction,

That enters my mouth through succulent suction.

I lick my fingers with every bite.

I do not care that it will keep me up all night.

I keep on eating.

And every single meeting

I grow closer to this food

 As if it were a person.

Our relationship will never worsen.

Our love is unconditional

Our bond is so nutritional.

With every single taste

Not one moment we share goes to waste.

If chocolate could not melt,

I would hold it in a warm embrace.

And if I were to decease,

I would be buried next to my chocolate bar

So that its taste would not be too far.

I write this as my last will,

This hand that writes is ever still.

For each dark chocolate kiss

Is a taste of eternal bliss.

Wine

Wine is the currency of my love.

I trade it for thrills with close friends.

With it, good times never come to an end.

Its vapors evaporate the worries

And with it, all troubled thoughts scurry.

And yet the thrill of the night stays in tact.

With wine, my vision becomes a shimmer

And my dreams become a glimmer

In my mind's eye.

They seem to be in reach.

 I sip from my wine and preach.

With wine, I do the things I say

And hope for the things I pray.

All for the purchase of a bottle of wine

And some shared time with friends.

All pleasure in moderation

For the exact sensation.

To this fermented fluid,

I owe a standing ovation.

Coffee

Dark, brown, soft and smooth
One sip and you are on the move.
You drink and go, no time to slow.
You become a one man show.

Endorphins collide, you skip from side to side
People wonder if you are Jeckyl or Hyde.
Coffee is not a myth
It is nature's highest lift.

I find respite in its aroma
My throat bathes in its heat like a sauna.
Calmness seeps in
As the coffee grinds steep in.

I am a slave to the grind;
Not one sip is left behind.
Serene but energized, content not stigmatized.
Coffee's powers have me mesmerized.

I drink and drink to bring me to the brink of creativity.

To overcome the powers of gravity.

To meet deadlines, to prevent disgrace,

To keep focused in this isolated space.

With coffee, I try to morph into something new.

To act and look back upon how I grew.

And if I do not I will be enraged

To know that I have only aged.

Coffee, my fountain of youth:

My dear friend, coffee speaks the truth.

Faster, faster, farther, and farther

Coffee sips are worth the bother.

However much I age,

Coffee will be with me through every stage.

I will savor every sip;

I will save every drip, drip, and drip.

The Elements

Walking down to the bridge,
Sun dips below the mountain ridge.
Winter falls, makes me gasp,
Is this breath to be my last?

No;
My bones freeze, becoming harder.
If not a human, I am a tree.
Writhing naked, with snow upon me.

I do not know where I go.
I continue to tread through this fluff,
Each stride a huff and a puff.

The wind is unrelenting
With no sign of abating.
I am trapped outside,
Nowhere to run, nowhere to hide.

Nature is my prison,

Changing weather is my rhythm.

I travel in search of an end,

Each element is a passive-aggressive friend.

I plod through this wrath

In search of a cleanse, a soothing bath.

What is my purpose? I do not know,

I squish the ground beneath my toe...

The elements moan

Through gurgling streams and grinding stone.

A friend of contradiction, elements of one

Create the storms that are to come.

I continue walking, standing taller,

Wishing these days would soon be summer.

Without love, without care,

Yet I have a pulse, I am aware.

A true companion is what I need.

The elements are a trap, I know their greed.

The Friend

It's been awhile since I've seen you my friend;
My time here is coming to an end.
This town is looking dark in places;
You can see it on our neighbors' faces.

Your mother Mary isn't looking her best;
Her hands are folded against her chest.
And your Father has made a deal with the devil;
He is turning the pub into hell.

It's been a long time since I've seen you my friend;
I am leaving once again.
Magdalene travels from church to church;
She prays for you on the altar perch.

Her heart grows heavy from the feel of your touch;
She misses you very much.
And with my face in the beer that I bought
I am drowning, absentmindedly, in thought.

What lies between us now is indifference;

Every relationship is a debt with a consequence.

And so we stay apart.

Once, when we were young, we had the heart.

How many years must go by until you and I are dead?

A gospel must be written down of all that we have said.

For memories fade and emotions die, but not the glory of our past.

Come back, my friend, this town is in need

Of a night that will not pass.

Come on back my friend, sing a song with me.

Many years go by, but not the ones we live free!

The Bar

In this dark hollow of a place

I see lust smeared across a person's face.

On another I see contempt;

Another does not know where his friend went.

I go to the bar for service;

Behind it is a bartender without purpose.

I extend out my hand with money

To which he is compelled to like sweet pollen.

But I am not the only fist dripping with cash.

Other arms are extended as if begging for mercy.

Asking for that oh so sweet nectar that heightens the sens-
es,

That flows into your mouth at leisure,

And increases the appetite for pleasure.

That liquid so divine

That makes you walk a shaky line

Between right and wrong

To the tune of a swooning song.

The fluid of which all purposes are united

And all sin is righted.

This bar is a hive

And on its nectar people survive.

Not together, but as one;

The dance floor is where the

Fermentation becomes done.

Dancing

Hands up high to the sky
Merriment that cannot die.
Smoke and beer, a whirl of cheer,
A beautiful face in the clear.

I hold its gaze in this people maze
Whirling about in a craze.
This moment should not pass;
I will not think of the past.

Music and glee, I dance, we dance, joyfully.
'Round and 'round a memorable sound;
Beat to beat with stomping feet;
Such joy, such laughter, that bouncing pleasure we follow
after.

I feel in place at this club;
I feel at home like a pub.

The Wink

That wink made me think that maybe she likes me.

It is a possibility that we lived in a moment of felicity.

That wink, wink made me think.

It brings me to the utmost brink of belief that maybe, just maybe, she likes me.

My dearest winker, that girl, I still think of her.

I think of her with my eyes wide open

And my heart is wide open

For her, my dear winker.

And for her I will search far and wide.

I now have a reason not to hide amongst the scenery.

This girl must belong with me, although a bit furtively.

That wink makes me think

As my heart sinks, as I fall asleep.

I promise to find her.

That wink was in a bar and there she was not far.

But now she is gone.

That girl who winked, who made me think.

The Ocean

I am drunk

To my lowest level I have sunk.

I am rolling beneath a tipsy wave.

Under which I brave.

Someone save me from these depths!

Raise me above the foamy crests!

For I am drowning in this sea

Below an ideal I cannot be.

I am at the noir of creativity,

Wishing to be in the sacred state of felicity.

In this state, I am scarred.

From the sacred state I am barred.

Time passes above

And escapes from me like love.

I inhale a deep breath

Only to suck in the ocean's depth.

The Finer Things in Life

A little wine, a little nibble

A little gravy dribbles down my cheek.

It is the finer things in life that I seek.

Fine restaurants and homey taverns,

Places far from dark, mildewy caverns.

A little light, a little darkness,

A little smile from a girl with a diamond necklace.

A little music, a little touch,

A playful dance, what a hopeful romance.

There is no such thing as luck,

But there is such a thing as chance.

Opportunities pass in a glance,

Such as the hopeful romance.

This time only twice.

The finer things in life make me smile.

This time on earth is worth wandering for a while.

I take her, this beautiful and fine life by the hand

And I am brought to another land.

I see things which at one time I did not understand.

The picture suddenly becomes one,

And even my wandering confusion is overcome.

But once I held her hand,

Time passes and this fine life crumbles to sand.

A little light is left before the night

And I fall asleep with the fading of the light.

I only need a little bit of the finer things in life

To fall asleep.

The House

It was willed

For it to build.

And build it did

On a foundation of sobriety.

For that one it was built.

Nail after nail,

The hammer could never fail.

It never stopped until every piece was placed.

It never stopped,

Never stopped banging.

Now, there it stands,

Silent and grand.

A monument of material,

A hollow soul.

That is all there is of life.

The one, the hammer, the house.

That is all there is.

A bunch of houses.

The Train

A train comes through;
It only comes by once a year.
My body starts to tremble
When I see it in the clear.

It's lifting dust, rushing down the track;
There is one seat in the back.
And when I'm ready, I take that spot
Put my life up in the rack.

There are people in this world
Who will miss me when I'm gone.
And there are those who have seen my shadow
Growing much too long.

My camp fire is dimming down;
Light becomes ashes in the end.
The train's engine is blowing smoke
And the track starts to bend.

Looking out I see the houses
Getting smaller from behind.
This train keeps pushing on,
There is no slowing on this line.

No conductor, not another soul
Upon this moving train.
I would turn this track around
For the love within my vein.

But this train goes 'round and 'round
It only comes by once a year.
It charges like the future
Its whistle's ever near.
Making choices, hearing voices
From the depths down below.
My heart keeps on beating fast,
Can someone make it slow?
And there's a girl, with love in her arms
And flowers in her hair.
Passing by I watch her cry
Our love turns to thin air.

The Sistine Chapel

People come and go

To see the work of Michelangelo.

His flay droops from the hand of a saint on Judgement
Day.

He said only God gives form to the ideal body.

People come and go,

Pretending they know Michelangelo.

The angels and samaritans are glorified and well

While the lost and wandering are pulled into hell.

My body trembles and droops as I gaze;

My head is swimming in this chapel, this symbolic maze.

There are paintings of martyrs who have come and passed

And still the images of them last.

My hands tremble giving form to truth,

For even I have fear of being flayed.

I wish to live a life that was not merely played.

People come and go

And see the flay of Michelangelo.

They see, but do they know?

People come and go but do not wait;

Do they see the outline of their fate?

They come to see Michelangelo

But as quickly as they come, they turn to go.

If I were to stay at a church

I would stay at this one.

To see what my soul would become.

But Michelangelo glares at me so,

So much beauty, I have to go.

I am merely dust drifting in his presence

I am blown away.

Depression

Pressing depression,

Every sentence is a regression

Back to depression.

Every thought closes the space,

Puts me into place.

There was a doorway I chased

But it was erased.

Too late for my escape.

Words are my only escape.

Depression,

The ultimate regression.

The shriveling of intellect

Is the symptom of emotional neglect.

I have to dissect thoughts themselves.

I keep a record of them on fake plastic shelves.

This place is where I document my disgrace.

My trophy, the lines of stress on my face.

I try to bang down the blank, white walls.

Make them fall.

But even my force is silent.

What is left is the depression of my intent.

Drifting On The Sea

I am drifting,

Drifting on the sea.

Where nothing matters to me,

Or you.

Not the machine.

Not even time itself.

Thoughts pass under me

Like the waves,

Massaging my back.

This is why you and I

Drift on the sea.

My eyes close

But the light is bright;

I see through my eyelids

The warm, yellow sunlight

Bathing my body.

Yes, the sun is there.

It has to be.

Nothing matters

When I drift on the sea,

All that matters is me.

I hear the salty tide beat upon the shore.

Its melodic rhythm makes me snore.

I am asleep, then awake.

Asleep, then awake.

I am drifting for its own sake.

No love or care

Just the smell of salty air.

The sea slowly separating me

From rocky, sandy reality.

Time drifts into the setting sun

The moon rises, the day is done.

Then another,

And another.

And I am still drifting,

Drifting on the sea.

The cool, smooth waves

Pass beneath me.

Nothing

Nothing is what I see

A darkness that cannot be.

Forms struggle

To take shape

Even sentences

Fall

And break.

Icicles

Slowly dripping from the ceiling

Fall on my head

And numb feeling.

An abyss

My mind is a mist

That rolls over hills

A picture that remains still.

But there is a becoming,

An expansion

My mind is a mansion;

That keeps on filling up the space

Until there is something, a place.

I can be God,

Creating shapes at will in the fog.

The shapes take form at my pleasure

At my command, at my leisure.

I have control,

Even of morality itself, I am a self-determined soul.

Behold the product of my prison

Read to the beat of nothing's rhythm.

There is tragedy in being;

Close your eyes and see nothing.

Reality is a disguise.

 Nothing is to see without understanding.

To walk towards something without meaning,

But to keep creating and taking shape;

Make the words and thoughts stick like tape.

From nothing I created something;

I am father; I am king.

The Authority Of The Nomad

I am destined to the fringe

The outskirts of reality to which I hinge.

No daring souls wander on this edge

For fear of falling off its shaky ledge.

The only authority, the only soul here

No one approaches, no one is near.

In sheer defiance I hold fast

Each step may be my last.

But alone on this edge I still remain;

I create my own course, this journey so insane.

I am the only life in this wilderness,

The only authority in this forest.

My only necessity is to consume

Every fruit I eat, picked too soon.

In my travels I am aware, not living

No love am I giving.

My most precious gift is my wisdom

But no one is here to listen.

The only authority, the only one here
No one approaches, no one is near.

I peek from the trees to the mountain of interaction.
I no longer climb that mass of distraction.
With no goal to set my aim,
I am free from pressure of obtaining fame.

I travel aimlessly wherever I go,
Are you not impressed with this show?
You follow like a drunken crowd
Stepping behind me, curiously, not loud.

Look upon my life!
Can you see my strife?
To have no purpose but to travel
To let physicality and thoughts unravel.

I am a slave to fluidity,
Caught in the snare of serendipity.

If not a traveler I am lost at sea,

Lying above the waves that pass beneath me.

Time passes without control

Stealing the essence of my soul.

If I could wrestle it, I would pin it down.

Gladly, I would watch it drown.

But to enact violence

Would break my silence.

A veil which I cannot lift.

I am on a course, it cannot shift.

The only authority, the only one here.

No one approaches, no one near.

And so I travel on the fringe

The outskirts of reality to which I hinge.

Occupy My Mind

I need to occupy my mind

With something I cannot find.

Something that will take up space

Something I cannot replace.

The emptiness in my mind

Needs something I cannot find.

Thoughts in and out my ear

With each passing year.

Fill up my mind

With something new,

Knowledge teaches me how to do.

Thoughts teach me how to be.

I have the idea of being free.

That is what I want to know,

Something to fill up my mind,

Something I cannot find.

Something that teaches me how to feel

That every moment I live is real.

Pour your words into my mind

Before I start going blind.

Simplicity

Simplicity is a quiet riot,

The forced organization of chaos.

It is the apprehension of veritas,

The beginning of my civilized life.

The break in my authority.

Yet I gain one thing and lose another.

Loss of many for the sake of the few.

Loss of color for blank space,

Loss of wants for needs,

Loss of conversation for quiet,

A stutter-less silence.

I am in a cafe, coffee in hand,

Looking out the window.

A simple life is one without plot,

The past is forgotten.

Except for love,

Of that I am afraid.

Love is a burning house, complication remade.

For now, I sit in my coffee shop, coffee in hand.

I smooth the surface of the cup.

This I can understand.

Part II
Rage And Other Discontents

Rage

I am of the age

That I should rage.

Bring my life to its next stage.

I am of the age

That I should find purpose

And not merely scratch the surface.

To not accept things the way they are.

To not let my dreams glisten from afar.

I am of the age

Where I should seize the moment,

Shun the past, and hold the future in my grasp.

I let my will loose and charge into the fray

So I can live the next day.

Rage today, let not my course go astray!

The Raging Alcoholic

The raging alcoholic

Runs through the street.

Everyone looks at him.

"That good bastard!"

They say.

And they themselves

 Jump into the fray.

The raging alcoholic

Dances through the streets

In a fervor he yells and greets.

He greets the sidewalk itself.

This good man

Is better than

A politician with a plan.

He is a scene,

You know what I mean.

He cannot hold a conversation,

But he is a sensation.

What is there to do
About the raging alcoholic?

Will he end up in jail?
People would like to hear the tale.
They gode him on
As they dance wildly into the fray.

Maybe he will die
He'll give a jump a try.
And there in his casket he will lie.
And we will all kneel and pray
And always remember that day,
That day he raged in the streets.

I feel sorry for the good man.
Surely he will learn their plan.
For now the raging alcoholic jumps in the streets
Saying hello to everyone he meets.

Exit The Machine

I enter the machine, the jaws of creation.

I enter the body and claw at the sensation.

I enter the machine, the concrete jungle

And speak words to shield me from struggle.

 I fight with beauty in the heart of this city, this machine

And my creation is a scream.

A scream of perfection with direction

A scream that swells above its cogs and toggles,

Its switches and glitches its complication and self fascina-
tion.

Its wires and concrete are my intention to defeat.

Its horns and whistles against which my soul bristles.

Its smogs and its fumes my lungs unintentionally con-
sume.

I create something simple and gorgeous to cut above this
machine

To smash against its jaws.

To become the antithesis of its creation.

Perfection and beauty rolled into one.

I rise as the North Star and crash into the Sun.

Summer

A mirage

A woman with a corsage

With sweat on her chest

And silk on her breast

A wedding puts bestiality to the test.

Words and sentences melt

Or rather sweat into each other.

 Like slummer.

I slumber at my friend's house on weekend nights

Girls walk by my closed door with their tights

Off.

But nothing can hold back summer.

Wavy and hazy days

Go by in different ways.

Fireworks bang out in the distance

The air is beat back without resistance.

 Girls on the beach bounce by in bikinis

Boys watch pretending to pass balls and beanies.

Sun rays bounce off my sweating brow

A parched throat tells me I need water now.

The heat turns the city into a jungle

Buildings seem to melt not crumble.

 Summer simmers into the night,

A hot blackness that wraps tight.

Coming again and again with every first light.

Marooned

I am an island,

Surrounded by emptiness as far as the eye can see.

I am a muffled beat

Made by the tapping of my feet.

I wish to dive into the empty depths that surround me.

But how can you go towards something you cannot see?

Fear is my anchor;

Holding me down, I cannot look around.

My old masters are gone;

As if I have done something wrong.

They planted words that grow in my head.

They remind me that I am not dead.

Words like integrity, trust, and responsibility.

They did not tell me about an emptiness like this.

Like ivy that slowly suffocates a tree.

This silence and singleness strangles me.

With the old masters

I could string a sentence together.

And they would pluck them,

Make them resonate and reverberate throughout the room.

The words and sound have died so very soon.

I am an island; I am marooned.

The Rat

Give me back my snack you filthy Rat!

Or I shall come at you with my bat...!

Where are you now?!

I just saw you beneath my brow!

I heard you're little prattle

And then my table, I heard it rattle!

For now I keep my bat on its rack

No doubt in my mind, you will be back...

And when you come back, Rat

I will spar you tit for tat!

For now I go back to bed

So I can rest my head.

I swear, Rat...

I dare you to come back.

Blue Collars And White Collars

Which one should I wear?

The blue or white collar?

Comfort or fit?

This one scratches me a bit.

This collar will get me a dollar.

This one will buy me an hour.

One is snug, the other is fitting for fancy offices

 Or a plush rug.

Like sentences, clothes evoke a style.

Some play the part of the rank and file.

Some are worth staring at for a while.

Some are distinguished above the rest

And stand out like a wave's foamy crest.

I choose to wear clothes

Like I wear my sentences:

Bold and inspiring,

The style never tiring.

The Commute

Damn man, get out of the way!

There are things to you I would like to say.

 But not today, not no way,

I am driving to work, to get my pay.

It's early in the morning and without warning

Someone drifts into my lane.

I honk and yell, "Are you insane?"

How I wish I could fly a plane.

Driving can be cathartic;

 During my commute, everyone is a target...

You do not want to be at the end of my fender bend.

Damn lady, get out of the way!

There are things to you I would like to say.

But not today, not no way I am driving to work to get my pay!

I drive everyday into this fray.

One whole hour and my mood goes sour.

One more day and I swear I'll quit!

But it's not the first time I said I would.

I am a metallic ball of fury when I am in a hurry.

All you cars in front, scram and scurry!

My acceleration should make you worry.

Everyone has to drive to work...

Oh, if we could all take the train.

 But I guess the experience is too lame.

 So I keep on commuting

Although to a cop, my car is probably worth booting.

My Stone

Up and

Down the mountain.

Up and

Down.

My stone is in tow

Wherever I go.

Night after night, day after day,

Minutes melt into each other,

Becoming a solid block of time,

My stone.

I push it up the mountain, alone.

When I reach the top

I look back down

And I do not remember every step.

Every time I went to my job.

Every time I walked through the grocery store,

Picked out boxes of cereal,

And said hello to the clerk.

Up and up

Down and

Down.

Pushing this stone around.

This block of time

That is only mine.

Up and up

Down and

Down.

There is Sisyphus, dead, on the ground.

No one knows what he found,

Going up and down.

But you and I are him.

Day after day, night after night,

Pushing our block of time around.

Up and up

Down and

Down

Pushing without stuttering a sound.

I cannot stop

Going up and up

Down and

Down

I like it a lot

I cannot stop

Going up and up,

Down and

Down

I just like it

And so do you

That is all we like to do

We, the unconscious heroes.

The Highline

People walk by naked

And flow unabated on the Highline.

They squeeze through its tracks in droves

Apartment windows perched like crows.

And that one is the one who knows

That lucky apartment dweller.

Trees and steel balanced

Art and construction meld into a stance.

These elements were not brought together by chance.

Rather, an urban Renaissance.

Thanks Bloomberg,

Of where you are I have not heard.

To some Americans, the Presidency is just a word.

Don't park it, walk to the Chelsea Market.

Smell the food

A culinary interlude.

Wander through the aisles

Travelers clad in hipster styles.

Rent goes up all the while.

Sometimes, people walk by and grunt

Their shoulders are forceful and blunt.

Especially at the spoken name of Trump.

But on the Highline,

Leave all political divides behind.

Leave behind the daily grind.

Leave all your troubles on the ground.

You can breathe and look around.

There is time, so much time

On the Highline.

Money

The paper under which I toil

Is money, man's unfriendly foil.

Money flows, comes and goes

Where it belongs, nobody knows.

The piles exchange, the bets rearrange.

Money is, to say it softly, the relative we try to estrange.

It plays in the arena we gamble

And fuels the political ramble.

Bankers themselves believe cash is king

Except where it is not doing anything.

It sits in caverns in piles

In stinking heaps that smell like bile.

The sight of it makes some smile.

 Our bodies wither away all the while.

Money, the means to an end that banks love to lend.

It is the friend I love to send

Away.

Money, buy me time, sell this rhyme... And I will wait,

For you to bring food to my plate.

Money, let me use you, but not throw you away

I cannot forget you the very next day.

The Ice Cream Man

Whenever I hear the ice cream man go by I cry,

"Why can't I be that guy!?"

All you do is drive and smile

Put that jingle on for a while

And everyone comes running to you.

You hand out savory sweets, that's all you have to do.

That jolly jingle makes my eardrum tingle.

And the ice cream man does it single!

All on his own,

He goes about his day without a tear or groan.

All for ice cream, such a delicious treat,

We all at one point are bound to meet.

The future is bright for the ice cream man

Everyone would like a cone in their hand.

Like Santa without the naughty or nice list,

You are his friend.

Just come running with money in your fist.

The ice cream man keeps driving about town.

He seems to be there whenever I turn my head around.

How my mouth waters for the savory cream

And how happy I am that he is not a dream.

I walk to him and ask for a cone.

He says, "Be careful when you walk alone."

I eat my dainty treat

And see that the ice cream man is gone.

And already, so is my ice cream.

What is sweet does not last for long.

Beauty

Beauty is a thin film
That covers the horrors of age.
Peel it back and behold,
All misgivings are revealed.

With some, you are better off concealed
For there is no understanding
Without this shield.
Covered in this film so thin
Your true intentions are hidden within.

But if you are to wear such a mask
You are safe to tell me, I won't ask.
My only intention is to know
And I promise I will let you go.

What I want to know is your true self.
To be reassured I was not talking
To someone else.

The Queue

There was a girl I knew

Who stood in the queue.

Waiting for a guy she knew.

He never came

There was no one to blame

Except the lovers who stood in front of her.

No fair man came to comfort her.

So she was alone by my side.

Nowhere to run, nowhere to hide

Except for me, of me she could confide.

I drained her eyes of the tears

Of which she wept

I promise you, they were kept,

Though she was a girl I never met.

For she was a girl in need

Of whom I agreed.

And I brought her back to the queue

To wait for the fair man she knew.

Love Not Yet Ready

Love, hold my hand steady, I am not yet ready.

Love, think fast, make this moment last.

Love, speak to me so I can hear.

Love, come close to me so I can feel you near.

 But still, my love, I am not ready.

I am frustrated that my hand cannot stay steady.

Frustrated that I don't know where to go,

Where to funnel my passion in a glorious fashion.

Love, show me the way, tell me the things I should say

And I will stay. I will be steady and ready.

Virgil

Virgil became my guide

He religiously attended to my side.

He knew much more than the books I own

His wisdom sliced through the great unknown.

Then, as soon as he came, he disappeared.

Why?

With him I could set my aim

And he would do the same.

But now his spirit is dead.

No sign of destiny shines ahead.

"Some help was he!"

I note sarcastically.

Who has ever even heard of Dante?

That bloke of which he spoke

Needed help...

Maybe he went back to him.

Or maybe he left because I have no love.

No passion fills the void of my heart.

There is nothing here but a wandering soul.

I admit this with regret

I will find purpose, just not yet.

My options are so depressing

That I have to keep digressing.

For Virgil is dead to me.

He once was my guide.

Sigh...

Is there another who will walk by my side?

Is there a friend for me with intentions true

Who can tell me kindly, what to do?

Who knows that heaven can be a place on earth

And knows what every choice is worth?

Who or what will fill this void in my heart?

It is filling up with rage

And turning the dark green color of jade.

'I Am None' And The Prophets

I have made it to Jerusalem,

I am at the Wailing Wall.

"Which man is the fountain of this land?

Is there life after death

By smelling his holy breath?

I speak to this authority of most high.

Tell me, who am I?

No one, I confess I am None.

My authority is overblown.

Look at the discourse that I have sewn."

Suddenly, a robed man appears in my midst

With gashes on the back of his fists.

"Silence!" he proclaims,

"Have faith!

Your hour is getting late.

Darkness will surely be your fate."

"Jesus, you have taken so much pain

How can I do the same?

Is my self doubt to blame?"

"Nomad, I am an inspiration

My believers are the standing ovation

To my death.

Fully man, I took the responsibility,

Fully God, I forgave.

Not only so that people would behave,

Show them that they can be more.

The New Testament is not just a book you find in a store."

At which point Muhammad appeared,

"You see", he said,

"Man has a propensity to slavery,

To abuse the poor, to shun the sick.

They would accuse a woman of theft

And ignore the morals of leniency and decency.

Come Nomad, and believe me,

I will give you direction towards a life of moral perfection."

Then, Abraham appeared, the first of the prophets.

"There is one God, dear Nomad,

One God above,

One God that we love.

This is the covenant,

Not simply an ark, but a belief we hold in our heart.

Believe him and all else will follow suit.

Shun him, and live alone."

To this I asked, "What should I do?

 Is there a commandment that unites all of you?

Time is short so your declarations are abridged,

How can I share an epiphany or experience I have never lived?"

They stared and looked at each other and in unison they replied,

"Love God and love your neighbor".

And Abraham declared, "Can't you see?!

This is how you live in community!"

The prophets stared at me.

Their shining eyes searching my soul,

Ascertaining how I lost control.

I can see the truth in their eyes, in their worn out gar-
ments.

Years and years of proclaiming testaments people could
not believe.

I am still skeptical of faith and love so I motion to leave.

I step back and bow, "May my intentions to follow this
never waiver."

We departed and I walked through the cobbled streets of
Jerusalem,

The containment of my spiritual asylum.

But I run back to the Wailing Wall and I shouted,

"I am looking for love, I just cannot see it in the God
above!"

Eros

Not just I, but thou, I want you now,

In the deepest sense of eros.

I want a beauty that can make sense of my life

Not just I, but thou, I want you now.

I multitask and take off my mask

And in your spirit I bask.

For a moment, the sun shines

And all of your shape is defined.

To possess you within myself is a form of self defense.

I do not mean offense.

I see beauty in you

And what you say is true,

Even your white lies.

All of our ethos, eros, logos and pathos should meld into one,

And that is what our souls become.

Not just I, but thou, I want you now.

Blank Faces

A blank face stares at me like a wall

Behind it there is nothing at all.

There is no emotion that sprouts from within

The head is nothing but an empty bin.

These blank faces are everywhere

I am the subject of their stare.

Their glowing indifference

Is a tragic act of self-defense?

Meanwhile,

The world crumbles before them

Like a flower breaks from its stem.

How can such beauty break before their open eyes!

Their stares must be a disguise!

And still the flower breaks from its stem

Its beauty falls before them.

A true tragedy has occurred

And I can do nothing but pass on the word.

Pictures On Screens

Pictures of me and you

That we look through.

Brief moments of unknowing connection

Hearts and likes force the social direction.

Show and tell

No need to spell.

Screens are the glue to our gaze

Look at you trapped in the maze.

Look at me, see the same

There is no one we can blame.

Reality is the haze in our background

People's footsteps are just sound.

There is no space for words in pictures.

No room for black scratches on a blank surface.

But there is fear in me to put these words down.

Who will stare at them?

Who will see the image of their meaning?

Who will look around

At the footsteps that were just sound?

What will happen when you and I look at each other and speak?

Just speak?

For now we are comfortable to stare,

To not be self-aware.

The pictures on screens

Of me and you

We, the unknowing minds look through.

Waterfall

If only

I could

Speak.

So much information

Bombarding me

Like a waterfall

Crushing me,

Drowning me.

So many words

Without meaning

I forget

How to think.

Commercial Break...

I cannot

Start

A conversation.

Commercial Break...

What was I doing?

Love?

Panic.

Fidgeting,

Where am I?

Who

Was that?

Where are my keys?!

Oh, here.

My...!

Phone!

There it is.

I found

Commercial Break...

...it.

I found

The words

To describe.

I like words

That don't hide,

Like rhymes

"Stick-out" words.

Words

Are my anchor.

My sanity, holding

The conversation

In my mind

In place.

Commercial Break...

I like

Words

From within me.

They have

Context

Or plot,

They are not

Easily forgot.

Those words

Speak.

Entrap you

In conversation,

A sort of sensation

Or effect.

These words

Return my intellect.

They are

Commercial Break...

My beauty

My picture

And frame.

Their meaning

Does not

Always look

The same.

And that is why

I have

To speak

To you,

Thou.

Commercial Break....

In spite of

This

Waterfall.

Breaking The Silence

Please talk and walk in words with me

Tell me what we should be.

Let our conversation lead

In spoken words I believe.

Direct your eyes at mine

Your face is one of a kind.

Break the silence, break the world displayed on your
screen.

Talk to me and you will know what I mean.

You and I are not meant to only seem.

Talk to me about what is true,

The art of conversation teaches us how to do.

Engage with me in elocution,

This will bring our problems to a resolution.

Only then, when you remove your face from your dream

Will you understand what I mean...

Yes, silence can be broken,

Syllables can beat, shake and break open.

Conversation is like stone,

That we carve, make our own.

This is our true craft.

The News

I know the news,

All of the hyperbolic headlines:

School Shootings! Mental Illness! Deception! Greed! War!
Refugees!

All of them ask for attention.

All of these problems fade away

When you turn the page.

All of those people gone.

I continue wandering from page to page.

I read about studies,

Studies about chocolate.

Those make sense.

Other articles become my kindling.

I watch the flames consume them

The melting ink, the burning words

Turn to smoke

Like an incense of hope.

Maybe tomorrow the news will be better.

Maybe tomorrow the headlines

Will say,

"Hello, how are you?"

And a hand will reach out from the black print

And shake mine.

I watch the newspaper burn.

I keep the article about

The study of chocolate.

A Cure For Indifference

Someone find me a cure for indifference;

Find me a remedy of consequence.

 Find me a way to be free

Without bending my knee.

Find me a way to act

Without doing wrong

 Or singing a profane song.

Find me a way to find pleasure

Without wasting away at leisure.

Find me a way to give

Without forgetting how to live.

Find me a way to care

In spite of knowing about poverty and despair.

I know it is always there and yet we all breathe the same air!

Find me a way to know

How to make a garden grow.

Find me a way to invite someone over for supper.

Find me a way to ask without a single stutter.

Find me a cure for indifference.

Alone

I sing a low tune when I am alone.

I walk through dark, moonlit fields

And I think of you when I am there.

If only our hands would touch

But not too much.

Our hands should close

Around a rose.

But you are not here.

You are the shadowy figure in my nightmare.

You are the shimmery apparition

Which I interact with in discretion.

You should teach me how

To share a space with another.

To walk step in step,

And may I not forget my lines,

The ones that bind me to others in hard times.

You should teach me how

To interact and to subtract

The awkward phrases

And replace them

With forgiving praises.

But I am alone

And I have not grown.

I am sinking like a stone.

Words, please rescue me!

It is said that to love someone

Is to see the face of God.

May I be struck by such a face

Like a shock to a lightning rod.

Regret

How can I forget

The things that I regret.

Troubled thoughts scream out loud,

And follow me like a shroud.

Regret is misery and mystery

Two things I cannot let be.

But these thoughts are not me,

Without them I am free.

I want to show more of me,

To contribute to the land of plenty.

But I cannot if thoughts are detained

And will is restrained.

I want to speak

Or else my thoughts will fester and wreak.

Speak and let be!

This regret is not me!

To paint the sky with color

Is a pleasure like no other.

To run through fields like fire

Is my utmost desire.

I want to see the world glow

From the excitement of my show.

And then, only then

Will God know

That heaven can be a place on earth.

Hope is the cure, of which I am sure...

 Let me put an end to this unending grief,

Silence my regrets!

Climate Change

It is only in disaster that we find relief

Only in tragedy do we find grief.

Accidents are inevitable,

Scientists say they are predictable.

Tragedy is the catalyst of human reaction.

Catastrophe is life giving distraction.

There is no solution to pollution

Without a tragedy to manifest;

So we let it happen.

I am not proactive

There is no incentive to be reactive,

To keep death at bay.

The environment degrades as they say.

We let cars and factories precipitate the disaster.

This would cause anger...

But you cannot see the danger.

Refugee

As always, I have to travel to another land
A place constructed by another hand.
Even with a promise to contribute,
My legitimacy is in dispute.

My passion has no direction,
So I travel with discretion.
My survival is at stake;
My own fate is what I make.

My goal is to be
A person who is free.
It is not my own decision
To be a refugee.

I have to swallow my pride;
There are enemies from which I hide.
I must make them think I'm gone,
Or better yet that I died.

To rise up in a Renaissance

 Is a dream, rightfully mine.

I am forbidden to celebrate such a moment so divine.

Each place that I find refuge in,

A new story will begin.

But in an estranged state

Is how I have always been.

To find love is to know

What is closest to your heart.

A self-sustaining love is what I seek

In a land which I will never part.

Bunker Hill

I am perched upon the obelisk of great sacrifice.

The view is grand and does suffice.

For all those fallen heroes

Their enemies now number zero.

Though they have died,

We continue to climb

And not one of the fallen souls we leave behind.

Their sacrifice was laid upon the ground,

Laying a foundation for this obelisk to abound.

This history sleeps quiet on Bunker Hill.

The story of soldier's actions go beyond human will.

They did not shoot until they saw the whites of their eyes.

They were patient with pain and stifled their cries.

You can hear the thunder rumble...

Even this great battle was reduced to rubble

But not the story of their struggle.

Great sacrifice I remember thee,

For freedom to wander you gave me.

What begins in America does not end tragically,

New beginnings start happily.

I look out upon the Boston view,

And think of starting something new.

Now young families run about Bunker Hill and play.

In remembrance of America's revolution day.

The Bowling Ball

Every moment rushes towards us

Like a bowling ball,

Slipping down its glossy lane.

Every time, it *crashes*.

We, the white, thin, pins,

Are at the mercy of each moment.

Each bowling ball,

Every single time.

I watch the bowling ball

Shuttle back to the top of the lane.

Switching like musical chairs,

We are put into place.

I hope the bowling ball

Does not hit me again,

The impending doom.

The bowling ball,

Mockingly, slides down the lane.

Gliding, slipping, and shifting

Steadily gaining speed.

We, the white, thin, pins stay huddled together.

We are paralyzed, it must be fear.

Is it?

You too are still;

You too are a thin, white, pin.

But I still do not know.

Strike, after strike,

We all fall down.

The crash of a moment

Is always near.

Death

Is death truly inevitable?

Is it truly the dead end which time cannot bend?

Or is it a doorway to another path, shielded from life's wrath?

I am inclined to believe, so as not to grieve

That age is just a myth

And every day is a gift

Upon which my spirit lifts.

Why not be immortal?

Life is about life.

 I will step before the black hole no one can control

And I refuse to pay my toll.

At death's door, I wish to stand with a friend.

To that friend I will lend my hand

And we will walk through the door and out across the land.

Death is the black I wish to pierce

With a sword through its heart,

Tear the darkness apart.

See the light and do the right.

No more a Nomad I wish to be;

No more stranded on the sea.

 No more death! I wish for life!

I walk through the hurricane that is life.

To find happiness in the eye of the storm.

Hope

Hope;

The lump in my throat

That rises as other people gloat.

At the center of attention,

Hope is my emotional invention.

Hope;

To risk it all and break the sneering wall is my calling.

But it is the big step that keeps me stalling.

All eyes upon me, the gloating eyes.

 And gode me on they do.

Hope takes two, a person and the dream to be.

To be what other people want to see.

To walk charismatically through the crowd,

To walk with animation, to be loud.

I will lift my shroud.

I hope to do it now, someway, somehow.

And in process, hope is making heaven a place on earth.

We all know how valuable that is worth.

Vulnerability

What makes man great is his imperfections.

He overcomes weakness without direction.

Man determines his own fate without God's discretion.

He is free to make his own impression.

He is vulnerable, a doubled edge sword

Which he holds; He is his own lord.

The world is his to command,

Which trembles under his outstretched hand.

But what is subjected can bite back...

And man can find himself under attack.

Man looks out at the world and sees a sea.

He is engulfed in wandering people that look like me.

Nomads; an endless sea.

Rising and fading quietly and tragically.

The Statue of David

There he stands frozen;

He has not yet chosen.

The stone touches his hip,

Choked in his grip.

I stare and sympathize so,

For even I do not know where to go.

A kaleidoscope of emotions must blind him

As he stares down Goliath.

He and I want more than survival,

He and I want a true trial.

Caught between something great

And the safety of an escape,

The light in our lives shines so brightly,

There is no time for debate.

But there is time to glare,

Into our demons we stare.

The defiance etched on our face

Is the only stone a Goliath cannot deface.

For the time we do not have, we stand naked.

This is our pride, we flex our human form, we cannot hide.

Part III
The True Way

De Ja Vu

Does she love me? Love me not?

I don't worry because I forgot.

De ja vu, I can't remember

Maybe I saw her in September.

Time, is on my side

On its hour hand I glide.

I do loop-d-loops, I eat Fruit Loops

Then I see her pass me by.

She was staring right at me,

I watched her through the glass.

She looks like a Susie Lee,

I hope she'll come say hello to me,

Then dance with me, please dance with me,

See how I roll.

Pick me up off my knees

I'll take you on a stroll.

She takes me by surprise

I saw my future in her eyes.

Meanwhile, we follow fate

Through the window and out the gate,

Over hills and far away

To places I've never been.

Two comets shooting through the sky

Time passing in between.

She flashed through my mind

And I passed by hers.

I want to hear her heart

Beat against my chest

When we lay down to rest.

Looking into her eyes,

I see past her disguise.

Beat back to my chest,

Lay down to rest.

Does she love me? Love me not?

I don't worry because I forgot.

De ja vu, I can't remember,

Maybe I saw her in September.

Time, you ticking clock,

Let me nail you to a wall.

Ask me questions, I'll answer yours;

Tell me your secrets all.

The Kiss

Wet and soft like a water soaked cloth.

My lips caress her cheeks

And my love for her leaks.

It leaks out of my heart and drips off my hand.

I hold her so she can understand.

So she can understand the meaning of my touch,

That she is not just a crutch.

Her velvet lips sooth

Over my head they move.

Establishing a rhythm, a groove.

There is much understanding in a kiss.

An opportunity that should not be missed;

It is not just an item on the bucket list.

I have been silent ever since then,

Ever since that tender kiss.

Lady Liberty

Freedom is the kingdom to come,
To it I run.
 It is the idea I did not know was there
And now I breathe it in like fresh air.

Freedom is proclivity for creativity.
Freedom is the virgin with supple skin
And enormous pride hidden within.
 My eyes gloss her over
In her glow I recover.

I kiss her on the lips
And let just our fingertips
Touch.

Lady liberty cannot be restrained;
She is imagination unchained.
She is the bread of life that sustains.
Her presence glows and reigns.

On her bosom I rest my head.

In this moment I will remember what is said.

That freedom cannot die

As long as there is a soul to try.

Actions are immortal

And thoughts open a portal.

Freedom is my second love;

She is amnesia and dangerous leisure.

I must leave her for true love.

I must stay the path

And be wary of freedom's wrath.

We'll Be Fine

Love, I did not know what to do.
I was caught in the crossfire, the fire of our love.
Love, tell me something new,
Tell me we'll be fine.

Love, the world is spinning 'round,
Around your little head, the world is falling down.
Like flowers in your hair, you take me by surprise.
One look at you, I fall into your eyes.

I'm taking a walk around this park by myself.
The moon is shining, but not shining down on me.
Nothing but wind and snow swirling in the air.
Nothing but a shadow, Love, I want you here.

Looking for a better way to get my drift.
I can have any drink, but it won't give me that special lift.
The one I'm looking for is sitting right next to me.
There is not a better place I would rather be.

Been back and forth between heaven and hell.

Where my soul lies, the devil can't even tell.

But when I'm with you, Love, all this pain fades away.

There is not a better place I would rather stay.

I'm taking a walk around this town by myself.

I'm thinking of the journal I put back on my shelf.

It's filled with sorrow and a love that runs deep.

Maybe just words or a promise that I'll keep.

Your grace is shining down from the sun up above.

It's filled with your majesty and magic, a never ending love.

And still you're standing here in the cradle of my arms

Sometimes I wonder, what will I do wrong?

Good times come around then come to an end.

For a moment, you stop the clocks and make time itself bend.

And when you do, I'll be standing here with you.

Because staying here is all I want to do.

We'll be fine.

Fear Me When I Am Sober

I think it's over

When I am sober.

The celebration is not there

And I am aware.

Yet,

The red rover, red rover

Can send all his problems right over.

Fear me, red rover, for I am aware;

Clarity is right there.

It looks strange

When the view does not change

From the vapors of wine.

For once in a dark night,

My mind is fine.

For once in a dark night,

There is nothing to celebrate.

But for once in a dark night,

I do not hesitate

To write.

And everything is alright.

Yes, I am sober.

And all of my problems gloss over.

For once in a dark night,

Beer does not cloud

My sight.

For once in a dark night,

Everything is alright.

Even the red rover

Does not start a fight.

Red rover, red rover,

Send my problems right over.

Fear me now

For I am sober!

Give Me A Word

Give me a word I have never heard.

I will let the sentence unfurl like a flower.

In its beauty you may run and cower.

Feel the power of this stanza's indent;

The empty space is my intent.

Give me a word, a singing bird.

I let it tweet a song you never heard.

Twitter! Twitter! Its wings lift and flutter.

The sound spreads like butter.

Give me a word, a standing tree.

I make the bark look like me.

Give me a word, the open sky.

Blue until the day I die.

Give me a word, the sound of peace.

The noise that anarchy loves the least.

Give me a word, wide open space.

The look of freedom, a sacred place.

Give me a word, love.

Rhymes resonate the powers above.

Give me a word, destiny.

My dreams lie abreast of me,

Waiting for me to seize.

You can give me a word, any word.

Even one I have never heard.

I teach them to fly, just like a bird.

Rhyming

In good timing, there is rhyming.

Words and spaces

Are not worth nickel and diming.

For every word creates a cost,

Without a purpose it is lost...

On paper.

All books depreciate

But their words in context appreciate.

Some words are bound to meet

And those that do gladly greet.

Paragraphs are still frames of time,

Sentences are brush strokes, line after line.

And look, their color is retained

In every book that has remained.

These words are who I am,

A reflection to look at and understand.

And when I am gone from this world I braved,

This is the part of me that will be saved.

Privacy

I am free with privacy,

The only struggle is against me.

I am on an island,

No one else but me,

Free to be as great as I can be.

No one else to measure my accomplishments.

Greatness is my only intent.

Privacy is the time and space I invent

And the warm feeling of being home.

In privacy, I have had the best love

That was bestowed upon me from some fortune above.

In private are the words I mean to say

That no one else can take away.

In privacy is the love I give

When I find room to forgive.

Privacy is the time I spend knowing

All that the world is doing.

It is the time that I take to understand,

How to correct unfairness and right the bad.

Privacy is the time I take to prepare myself for the public eye,

Even if I have to show things that make me sigh.

In privacy was the greatest challenge I ever had.

To look myself in the mirror

Through good and bad,

Wandering as the Nomad.

Church

Under this steeple

Is an ark filled with virtue loving people.

They have promised to do penance

And become divorced from menace.

In charge is a priest

Who has sinned the least.

Or who at least is humble

To acknowledge his trouble.

This ark is sailing for heaven,

Sailing upon deadly, sinful seas.

In this church, I have carved out my spot.

Of my wandering ways, my peers have forgiven, but not
forgot.

But still my love and I hold onto this voyage true

To discover the promised land of which our younger souls
knew.

And with love by my side,

I may weather any tide.

The priest pounds at the pulpit

In the cradle of this ark so strong.

The promised land beckons, it will not be too long.

Surely?

Who knows...

I only follow where the sentence goes...

Good Ol' Aristotle

Temperance is a virtue;

A savory fat I have learned to chew.

And that is how I grew,

The middle road I walked through.

I did not see it at first;

I took a turn for the worse.

But then he told me to stay my course,

He saved myself from divorce.

He said, "Take the middle,

Not the extreme".

Through experience,

I understand what that means.

He opened up my mind

To what lies beyond.

The middle road you always take,

Like a marital bond.

Joy

Joy is not a mere toy;

It is the bread of life that everyone works for.

It is spoke of in tales of lore;

It is the emotion that feeds your core.

Joy is the emotion that puts a halo above your head;

It is the signal that your troubles are dead.

It guarantees that you speak the truth;

No need to hide the parts of you that were once lies.

Joy breeds life and replenishes the earth.

It is avidly sought after, especially after disaster.

It is the happiness that we cry out in tears.

It is the book that we keep on our shelf and read through the years.

The Practicality Of Dignity

The homeless, in a sense, were one of me.

Each one wondering who they should be.

They hold on dearly to their dignity

On brown cardboard.

They hold it on the street;

They show it to people, but only their feet.

They are not eye level to each passerby,

Yet they see the indifferent sigh.

The cold shoulder makes these words bolder.

There is practicality in dignity.

Those who pass do not know because they cannot see.

A life that lives is a life that can give.

A life that is sheltered is one that can forgive.

The life with a home is no longer alone.

A life with a friend shares stories that never end.

Building a home is our battle against fate.

Our limitless will to love and create.

The will to survive upon which we thrive.

When together only then

Do we feel alive.

When there is no money, there is at least empathy.

Imagining the way things can be

Is the power of hope and creativity.

The will to overcome pain and the greatest grief

 Is a sign of promised relief.

And what follows is the practicality of dignity.

Time

You cannot share it
But you can waste it.
You can divide it,
But you cannot conquer it.

It cannot walk
But it can fly by.
It is like the sun
Slipping across the sky.

It can be written down,
It can be erased,
But it can never stay in place.
Sometimes it is just water under the bridge.
Sometimes it is your car falling off a ridge.

It is love
Like a smothering hug.
It is hate
Like a heated debate.

We have tried to create it

By building machines

To save it

So we can live more,

So we have more

Freedom.

But like a hot air balloon

With too many holes to patch

It escapes us,

Slowly.

It is grounding us.

It makes us

Human.

Human As Can Be

Human as can be,
Our bodies the token of creativity.
Thoughts flow from our mind
And leave logic behind.

Human as can be,
Knocking arrows at objectivity.
And that is why we have authority,
The power of community.

Human is to be aware of sensitivity,
Of every single nuance,
Of how things are supposed to be.

Human is to order,
To create walls that border.
The pieces should just touch,
And not move so much.

To be human is to create,

To make decisions, not hesitate.

Accomplish something we call great.

To be human is to fail,

But in the end prevail.

Each obstacle is a gate;

We assail, assail, assail.

Smile

I have not seen it in awhile,

Your smile.

All of the rejections diminished your projections.

I hope not the curve of your grin

Where all our hope begins.

The expression that should remain in this concrete city.

Smile; stare for awhile and laugh.

It is laughter we follow after,

That we live ever after

Even after disaster.

Smile with me.

Stare at each other in the Sun.

Do you see what we have become?

Two souls united as one.

Two smiles dancing in the light.

Two smiles grinning into the night.

That smile allowing me to write.

A smile helps me produce;

Helps put these words to good use.

There is no excuse for unused words.

I let these words pass through my lips

And wrap them around your hips.

Then you smile like the sun,

Though you cannot be eclipsed.

My Fountain

When I thought I had no words left to speak,

I met you.

In you I discovered a spring

That I have built a fountain around.

Little by little, the fountain pulls up thoughts, ideas,

The precious resources that sustain my life.

The fountain itself becomes more ornate, sophisticated, and efficient.

I am wary not to use the fountain too much.

I wait and sleep beside it,

Waiting for the water to replenish.

When I see my fountain is ready,

I dip my bucket in.

There they are,

Lucid imaginations swashing around the bucket.

I have captured them.

I drink them, I become them.

I am becoming more of you.

This is our own circle of life.

When there are no words left to speak,

You will always be my fountain.

The Rain

Drip drop to the tick tock of the clock.

The comfort of rain.

Water streaks down the window pane.

The sky a dark, powerful grey,

Thunder banging out the day.

Rain and fog roll out across the sky.

The grass is wet, it has been too dry.

Drip drop to the tick tock of the clock.

Covers of my bed,

Rolled up to my head.

My eyes are closed.

I am at peace, not dead.

You can see my smile.

My thoughts sink into a warm darkness

As if tethered to lead,

And I still hear the drip drop to the tick tock of the clock.

In this calmness I can sleep.

This is the moment that I keep.

Mine forever, this is the ideal weather

That drips and drops to the tick tock of the clock.

Home

Nature springs forth from the ground;

How long will it be around?

Yet so beautiful I cannot forget it.

I do nothing but let it be,

Let it be the vitality I can see.

The trees reach toward the skies,

Punctured by eagles' cries.

The waters runneth over with fish,

So abundant that a net cannot lift.

I walk upon this path,

Undisturbed from human wrath.

Its soil warm and soft to the touch

And supportive like a wooden crutch.

The air is filled with pine,

A scent so sublime.

It wafts through the gaps of my nose

And fills the cavity of my lungs.

The mountains reflect the sun

Like a shining diamond.

Such behemoths cannot break

But in a moment I will climb them.

I head to the trees that lie at its base

And turn to the mountain's face.

The trail is uneven

But I push on,

My journey has a reason.

Stones crush beneath my feet

As I ascend the rocky face.

The buzz of insects disappears

As I ascend the mountainside.

Life disappears as I rise to the top.

With every effort, I leave behind a precious creature.

The climb becomes more lonesome, more burdensome on the heart with each one left behind.

I look out at the top and behold,

All life spreads me like a sumptuous carpet.

What life was once missing

Is now a view worth kissing.

The journey that was once filled with suffering,

Is now a homecoming.

Age

Stories are the lines on your face

That crinkle without disgrace.

The smile of your crows feet

Is the defiance of your heart beat.

This repulsiveness is true beauty that won't deplete.

The years you live are victories over the passage of time.

Every year, death draws near,

But your life is the solid statue that embodies death's fear.

An icon of God's image

That heaven receives,

Death cannot pillage.

You stand and blow out the candles;

This year was a fire, easily handled.

When you speak, you are the stage.

Your written words crystalize on the page,

This is how we know there is victory in age.

Mother

I was the apple of your eye,

With every move I made you cry,

For fear that I would die.

But risk is a matter of life that we deal with in stride,

And from which we should never hide.

With every move I will remember you

For bringing me into this world.

The stars are ever steady and prepared for capture.

And when my dream is ready to take,

Your name I will not forsake;

Our bond I will not break.

My dream I will obtain and it will live long in the memory.

Forever remember me, never forget me.

Forever will I be the apple of your eye,

May my sweetness never die.

Why I Wait

Some days

I wish the world were new again.

Like I experience it for the first time.

Like a first kiss,

Like the first time I wake up

And truly see the sunrise.

Now that I know the world,

It is too familiar.

The sensation of life

Has lost sensation.

Day after day

I desperately chase after some kind of feeling.

The present is never present,

Even when I share it with a ruby red sunset.

Its colors fade,

The brush of wind is softened.

Now, after so much chasing

I have become quiet

And still.

I wait for meaning, for sensation to come to me.

I wait for the kisses.

I wait for the conversation.

I wait for the sun to rise,

For its rays to seep through my closed blinds.

For the birds to cry out across the sky,

Screaming,"I am alive!"

And they do come.

They all come.

Making the world new again.

I realized

You only have to wait.

The Answer

I used to sleep in my stress;

I woke up taking tests.

Now they are over,

My life is an open space.

The emptiness stares at me

And I have found an answer.

I have discovered my life

Is like a pasture.

Everyday I wake up

To plant a new seed.

It grows and I watch.

Sometimes it is a willow tree,

Leaves unfurling gracefully,

Covering me.

Sometimes it is an apple tree,

Feeding me.

Sometimes I don't know,

So I let the day go.

But still the plants grow.

They are the answers

To all my questions.

They continue to be

Even when the world seems to fall around me.

I go to this pasture and watch the plants grow.

They know,

Staying still and spreading roots,

Making use of what they have.

And they have so much.

That is what I did not know,

That is the answer.

Love Can Never Be Alone

To the Dark I lost a friend,

In the Dark he saw his end.

In this Dark which is a hole,

A falling feeling you cannot control.

In the Dark there's nothing there,

Except for space and whirling air.

A solitude you cannot measure,

Yet you can feel with every tremor.

Farther, farther, falling faster,

My demise tipped by disaster.

Like a blow it hits your head,

It makes you feel like you are dead.

How do I know of such a hole,

That is a grave that traps your soul?

Because a girl pulled me back;

She gave me hope of which I lacked.

How strange it is...

She was somewhere within my midst;

I did not see her until we kissed.

It was then that we entwined

And she was one within my mind.

She is the love that flies above;

Through the air, like a dove.

She is the warmth within the cold

And shelters me when wind turns bold.

She is the treasure once covered up,

But now sits with me at every sup.

She is the sparkle in my eye,

Which makes me wonder and makes me cry.

She is the friend I never had,

Who joined me in good and through the bad.

She is the grasp that's always there,

When darkness falls and fills the air.

When I am lost she is the light,

Which shines all day and through the night.

When we are safe in our home

I confess to her finally,

"Love can never be alone."

If all I've said about her until this

Were comprehended in a single praise,

Now it would be too little to suffice.

I saw her beauty passing all our ways

Of understanding, and believe indeed

That He alone who fashioned her enjoys its fullness

From this pass I must concede

Myself more overcome than ever was

Trajedian or comic at the peak

Of difficulty: as the sun in eyes

That tremble weakly, so my memory

Of her sweet smile now robs the intellect

And leaves me at a loss. From the first day

I saw her face until this vision now,

My road to song has not been cut away,

 But here, as every artist, I must bow

To my last power, and cease to follow on

Her loveliness by signs in poetry.

— Dante Alighieri (1265-1321 AD), Paradise

About The Author

This is Liam Sullivan's debut work of poetry. Liam Sullivan resides in Eastchester, New York. He graduated from Providence College with a BA in Sociology and Economics. When he is not writing, he can be found wandering around places in New York City like the Highline or Central Park, buying coffee from Slave To The Grind in Bronxville, or running on the Bronx River trail. He is a math instructor at Mathnasium of Mamaroneck and Scarsdale. For comments or questions, Liam can be reached at the following email address: thenomadpoetry@gmail.com.